The

Entrepreneur's

Workbook

Table of Content

Disclaimer

No part of this workbook may be reproduced in any form or by any electronic or mechanical means, including information storage and retrieval systems, without permission in writing from the Authors. While every effort has been made to verify the information in this directory and ensure the validity and currency of the content, neither the authors nor their affiliates or partners assume any responsibility for errors, omissions or inaccuracies. All information contained herein has been verified as true and accurate at the time of publishing of this content.

Meet the Authors

Quinetta J.W. a native of Newark New Jersey but raised in the Carolina's. She is a Serial Entrepreneur that loves to Inspire, Empower and Educate. Her ability to grasp the concept of being a Entrepreneur came naturally. "It's in her Blood" She grew up watching the strong black women of her family being their own "Boss" owning business and being successful at doing it. They went from street vending to owning hair salons, corner stores, food trucks, and laundromats just to name a few, and yes, she worked at just about all of them at some point in time. But what she didn't realize at the time is watching, working and being a part of the process at such a young age molded her into the Entrepreneur she is today. Her inspiration to write" The Entrepreneur's Workbook" came from simply meeting and talking to Everyday people from different walks of life that are in business or have an Idea and don't know what it takes and how to get started.

Ashley J. born and raised in Trenton, New Jersey. She is a serial entrepreneur, she has an event planning business, a transportation business, and a consulting business. Just like her sister, Quinetta it's in their blood to be their own "Boss". However, Ashley's drive came from needing to be available for her children. Growing up she worked for all types of companies in all departments, she learned how to run a business from front end to back end working in the corporate world. In every place of employment, she was admired for her ability to lead and simplify work processes. After opening many successful businesses and assisting others in opening their business, she knew she needed to create a book that will assist others on their journey to becoming an entrepreneur

How to Use Our Workbook

This workbook was created with you in mind.

As a serial entrepreneur, we know firsthand how frustrating it can be getting your business off the ground. From funding to finding customers we've been through it all.

To make life a little easier for aspiring entrepreneurs we created this book to assist them in the process.

This book teaches you how to set up your business, so you can become legit and take advantage of what is offered to small businesses.

It also teaches how to establish business credit, so you will not mix personal with spending and it gives more spending leverage.

Even if you have bad credit, do not let it discourage you, this book teaches you how to build and rebuild your personal credit and credit score. Let's face it, credit matters. You cannot begin your journey of financial freedom with bad credit.

This book also gives you strategies on saving, budgeting, even marketing.

This workbook is setup into two sections, the first section is informative. The second section is interactive, here you will find the templates for you to utilize.

Business Plan

So, you want to start a business? All successful businesses started with a business plan.
We have created a basic Business Plan outline for you to begin creating your business plan. Use this as a guide to help you in the planning of starting and running your business. *(Remember this is just an outline to assist you in creating a business plan)*

Why do you want to start a business?

____

____

____

____

What does it mean to you?

____

____

____

____

What type of business do you want to start?

____

____

____

Business Plan Continued

Who is your ideal client?

____

____

____

____

What will you offer? Product or service?

____

____

____

____

Who is your competition?

____

____

____

What is needed to operate your business?

____

____

What will be your process of operating your business?

How to Start a Business

So, you have an idea and you want to make it a business!?

Follow this step by step guide and you'll be sure to make that dream a reality!

Step 1. Name your business

You must think of a name for your newfound venture, not just any name but a name that represents you and your brand. Once you think of a few names, you must check to see if they are available in your state. So, make sure you conduct intensive research when choosing a name, because you do not want to start the process and then realize you must change your name.

Step 2. Choose a structure for your business

Now that you have done your homework and chose an available name for your business, you must choose a structure for your business. The structure of your business is how you will run your business, there are 4 main structures to choose from. They are the following:

Sole Proprietorship: does not separate the owner from the business for tax and liability purposes. Ownership cannot be transferred; in the event of the owner's death the business is dissolved.

Partnership: involves more than one person and a partnership agreement that outlines their individual responsibilities and how money will be distributed is required. There are some tax advantages and owners may have personal liability.

Limited Liability: separates the owner from the business to a certain extent, LLC combines some benefits of a corporation with some benefits of Sole Proprietorship or Partnership. An LLC is dissolved when a member (owner) leaves, and members are required to pay their own Medicare and Social Security contributions.

Corporations: are separate legal entities that separate the owner's personal assets from the company, there are two main corporations to choose from:

(S Corp) owner is only taxed, based on distinctions made by the IRS

(C Corp) business is taxed separately from the owners

Be sure to speak with a tax expert to discuss the benefits of each structure to choose for your business.

Step 3 Apply for an EIN

An EIN is an Employer Identification Number and is issued by the IRS. There is no fee to apply for an EIN from the IRS.

If you are interested in establishing business credit for your company, it is ideal to not use a residential address. If your business does not have a physical location or if it is truly a home business, then you can purchase a virtual address instead. This is a vital step in establishing business credit.

Step 4 Register with your state

This should be easy because you have already done your research and made sure your name was available. Now you will have to register the business with the state where you want to operate your business. There is normally a fee for this, it varies by state and structure. If you are selling products, you may need a reseller permit as well.

Depending on your structure, you will need to have Articles of Organization or Articles of Incorporation.

Articles of Organization- outlines and separate an LLC, it is also known as certificate of organization or a certificate of formation

Articles of Incorporation establishes a corporation as a separate business entity, it is like the bylaws of the company.

Step 5 Open a Business Bank Account

It is imperative that you keep your business expenses and profits separate from your personal, which is why you need to open a business bank account. Be sure to do your research before choosing a bank to do business with. This bank account is strictly for business purposes only, do not mix

This is the account where you will receive revenue from your sales or services, it is also where you will pay bills and keep account of your spending. If you plan on taking out a loan, having a business bank account is needed.

Step 6 Create a Professional Appearance

As a business owner, you are your brand! You must always represent yourself and your brand in a professional way! You never know who is watching.

A Professional Appearance consist of a logo for your brand, a website, social media pages, professional email address (info@yourdomain.com), a telephone number, and fax number.

A logo identifies your brand, be sure to have one created once you decide on your name. The logo must represent your brand as well as stand out with creativity.

A professional website gives your brand and company an existence. In a society where social media is the biggest platform, an online appearance is needed. That's why it's imperative to build a website and social media accounts corresponding to your business. Online may be the first place your potential customer is introduced to you, and we all know first impressions are lasting impressions.

In addition to having an online appearance, you will also need a professional email address. Having a professional email demands respects, it lets your audience know that you are legit. Knowing that they have a way to contact and without seeing

It is also going to be needed when establishing business credit.

Congratulations! Your business has officially been set!

<u>Notes</u>

Business Names

Top 10 Names

1._____________________________

2._____________________________

3._____________________________

4._____________________________

5._____________________________

6._____________________________

7._____________________________

8._____________________________

9._____________________________

10._____________________________

Opening a Business Expenses

Filing Fees $_____

Business Account $_____

Website $_____

Domain $_____

Logo $_____

Phone & Fax $_____

Virtual Address $_____

Business Structure

Sole Proprietor

Pros   **Cons**

____

____

____

____

Partnership

Pros   **Cons**

____

____

____

____

Limited Liability Company

Pros   **Cons**

____

____

____

Corporation (C)

Pros

____

____

____

Cons

____

____

____

Corporation (S)

Pros

____

____

____

Cons

____

____

____

<u>Notes</u>

Notes

Marketing

For any business to thrive, you must market your brand well. Marketing is the heart of your business, it spreads your brand, boost your sales, and builds your reputation to gain new and returning customers.

You can have a great product or service, but without marketing no one will ever know about it. This can be detrimental for your business, because you will have low or no sales.

Remember marketing consist of advertising and promoting. In today's society the most efficient way to market is online, however you must have a plan and remain consistent.

We are not marketing experts; however, we do suggest planning monthly. Planning monthly will assist in keeping you consistent with marketing. Remember consistency is key to great marketing.

We have provided a template for you to use to assist in your marketing plan, this template will help you organize how you will market your business for the month.

Consulting with a marketing expert is highly recommended when you are ready to launch your business.

The template is to provide you a place to jot down what you will focus on and strategies to promote it monthly.

The templates will be at the end of this workbook in the activities section for you to use over a course of a year.

Credit Repair Made Simple!

Do you need to Repair- Rebuild & Establish Credit? Well look no further. This do it yourself guide is designed to provide you with all the information you need!

First and Foremost gather all 3 of your credit reports to get started if you have not received your three free credit reports for the year you can go to WWW.ANNUALCREDITREPORT.COM

Equifax, Transunion, Experian

If you have already received, your free credit report for the year, no worries when there is a will there is a way! Go to WWW.CREDITKARMA.COM & WWW.EXPERIAN.COM to receive your free credit reports YES FREE! Print all 3 Credit Reports. Now let the Journey begin!

***A credit report is a detailed record of your financial history**
*** A credit score is a numerical expression based on a person's credit file to represent your credit worthiness**

1. Your credit report is divided into a few main sections

    a. Personal Information
    b. Summary of Accounts-open, closed, charge offs
    c. Public Records
    d. Collections-Medical bills
    e. Inquires
    f. Creditors contact information

2. Your FICO credit score has five factors used to calculate your score
    a. Payment history 35% (paying on time is very important)
    b. Amounts owed 30% (carrying a high balance, having a lot of dept owed is a red flag)
    c. Length of credit history 15% (the longer the history the better)
    d. Type of dept 10% (good mix of different types of credit)
    e. New Accounts- Inquires 10% (too many will bring your score down)

Credit Repair Made Simple!

Soon… You have all three of your credit reports, right?

Printed?

If you answered yes, then let's move forward.

Now that you know what a credit report is and how your score is calculated let's dive right in!

Dissection- a very detailed analysis of a text or idea!

The 6-part dissection

A. Personal Information- Check the spelling of your name, address, ss number and make sure it's all correct. Highlight all errors of information. Spelling errors incorrect address etc.…

B. Summary of Accounts- Dissect all your account check for accuracy with amounts owed, payment history, account numbers, dates opened and closed. Check the age of the accounts. Are they over 7 years old? Make sure it's your account, CHECK, CHECK, & CHECK again. Highlight all errors and incorrect information.

C. Public Record- If you have a tax lien, civil judgment & bankruptcies you will find them in this section. Check all dates for accuracy, including docket numbers, court dates check status accuracy for paid or unpaid accounts. Highlight all errors and discrepancy and make sure all account is correct.

D. Collections- If you have an unpaid account that has been sent to a collection agency you will find them in this section check these accounts for accuracy with amount owed payment history dates and overall correct information. These accounts have been turned over by the original creditor and they are trying to collect on a dept. Highlight all the incorrect information on these accounts CHECK, CHECK, &CHECK again

E. Inquires- Have you applied for a new account? If so, you will find that information here. Check this information for accuracy. Have you given these companies permission to run your credit? if not Highlight all the companies that did not have your permission to check your credit.

F. Creditors contact information- In this section you will find phone numbers and address of the companies you have or had accounts with this information will be very useful when getting your financial information reported updated correctly.

NOTE: **These steps should be followed on all three reports. They may have information correct on one report and incorrect on another so dissecting each report is crucial to the process.**

Credit Repair Made Simple!

Soon… You know what a credit report is and how your score is calculated

You have your printed credit reports

Do you have all your errors/inaccurate information highlighted?

If you answered yes to all the above, then let's move forward.

In this area you will learn how to dispute all the erroneous information on your report. It's the responsibility of the Creditors and the credit bureaus to report accurate information, section 609 of the Fair Credit Reporting Act is a Consumer Disclosure section which is to provide for the protection of consumers against false and erroneous reporting. You have rights, so let's learn how to use them!

The Dispute- to disagree, argue or debate

A. Personal Information- All incorrect information need to be updated and/or removed to have your personal information updated simply send a Certified letter to the credit bureau with your correct information to update. Only keep your current address on file, also provide them with the details of the incorrect information reporting on your credit report and have it removed (Template Included)

B. Summary of accounts- In this section there are 3 different accounts you could have encountered with erroneous information that will need to be disputed. Open, Closed, & Charge-offs Depending on the discrepancy of the accounts you will have to choose the correct templet according to the account's situation. The most effective way to have a negative account removed from your credit report is with a 609 Letter sent Certified to the Credit bureau (Templet Included) This process may take more than one attempt, sample templet letters provided for each attempt.

C. Public Records-To tackle a tax lien, civil judgment or bankruptcies there are specific step to be taken. First you must contact the 8 third-party reporting agencies and have your consumer files frozen. You should suppress files as well. (Contact information for all agencies that, this must be done with is listed on the Directory page *). After suppressing and having your files frozen with the agencies then you're ready to mail your certified letter to the Credit Bureaus using the (Template Included) to dispute all erroneous information on your report.

D. Collections- There are two different type of collection accounts medical and non-medical accounts. The first step in disputing any collection is "Validation" if the account cannot be validated it has to be removed from your account. Send a Certified letter to the collection agency to have them provide you with the specific details needed for validation (Template Included) also send a Certified letter (609 dispute letter) to the Credit bureaus.

E. Inquires- Hard Inquires appear on your report when you apply for new credit or credit increases. If there are any companies that appears on your report as a Hard Inquire and you did not give them permission to pull your credit you can dispute by sending a Certified Letter to the Credit Bureaus (Template Included)

F. Creditor Contact Information-In this area of the report you will find all the creditors contact information including address this is very beneficial when making the necessary contact with Companies.

NOTE: There are 21 FREE Templet's provide with this book they will be sent to you via Email upon purchase completion an Email address must be provided to receive the link! wwwsquinique.com

Directory/Reference

Company	Phone Number	Mailing Address	Website
Experian	800-509-8495 877-284-7942 888-397-3742	P.O Box 4500 Allen TX 75013	http//www.experian.com
Transunion	800-916-8800 877-322-8228	P.O Box 2000 Chester PA 19016	http//transunion.com
Equifax	866-349-5191 800-685-1111 866-493-9788	P.O Box 740256 Atlanta GA 30374	http//www.equifax.com
ChexSystems	800-88-7652		www.checksystems.com
early warning services	800-325-7775		www.earlywarning.com
Tele check*	800-366-2425		http//www.firstdata.com
Microbial*	800-884-4747 888-222-7621		www.microbilt.com
LexisNexis*	888-497-9172		www.lexisniexis.com/privacy
Stage stream*	888-395-0277		http//.www.stagestreamllc.com /security-freeze
Advance resolution services Inc. *	800-392-8911	5005 Rockside Rd, Suite 600 Independence, Ohio 44131	
Credco CoreLogic*	877-532-8778		www.credco.com/securityfeeze
Innovis*	800-540-2505		www.innovis.com
Clarity services Inc *	866-390-3118		www.clarityservices.com

Credit Repair Made Simple!

Soon… You know what a credit report is and how your score is calculated

You have your printed credit reports

Do you have all your errors/inaccurate information highlighted?

Do you have all your letters enveloped and ready to go to the post office to send off via Certified mail?

Do's Don'ts & Facts

1. If your request is approved the credit agency will send you an updated copy of your credit report.

2. If your request is denied within 15 days of the date the investigation is completed the credit bureau must show proof of the information used to verify the items on your credit report if they can't it has to be removed!

3. *Warning* do not use the online dispute tool. It gives up the right to re-dispute that claim if the bureau makes a decision that is not in your favor all correspondence with the credit bureaus and collection agencies should be done via Certified Mail.

4. Keep all receipts and records of time and dates for sending and receiving letters.

5. After seven years negative history should fall off your report. Public records like bankruptcy could appear on your report for up to 10 years.

6. If the credit agency doesn't send you adequate proof, you have options. File a complaint with your attorney general CFPB (consumer financial protection bureau @ www.consumerfinance.gov/complaint.

7. Mail all correspondence Certified and keep a log of all transactions and dates.

8. Certified letters to the collection agencies or credit bureaus may have to be done more than once the key is to stay consistent and don't give up. They are responsible for reporting correct information.

9. Another tactic when repair your credit is being offered a settlement from a collection agency. This will be a great way to have a negative item removed from your report. When aggreging to pay off a dept by way of settlement to the collection agency have them agree to do a pay to delete (Templet provided) they are not obligated to delete but you can make this a part of your agreement just make sure it is all done in writing do not correspond via telephone to finalize a settlement

10. General statement being added to your account may not be helpful in some cases it's not something that I recommend, the statement can remain on your account after the account has been deleted. Lenders will only consider a statement if you're going through a manual review and in that case a statement should be submitted directly to them.

11. According to section 611 of the FCRA, upon request the bureaus must provide a consumer with a description of how an investigation was conducted no later than 15 days after receipt. If all else fails, suing the bureaus in small claims court may be the answer. Keeping good records are important.

NOTE: You will start to receive letters for the 3 credit bureaus and collection agency you have contacted. Read carefully all the information they send back, that will tell you how to proceed in the future whether it's to repeat the process or send a different set of letters remember if the bureaus have not shown proof of the information used to verify the items on your report it has to be REMOVED. Don't give up! You're on your way to making your goals a thing of the past!

Credit Repair Made Simple!

Soooo… You're on your way to having a positive credit profile!

Now that you have started repairing your credit and updating all your reports.
Now is the time to start building or rebuilding your credit in conjunction to repairing it listed below you will find a few suggested ways to build a positive history.

Building & Rebuilding Credit Options!

1. Pay everything on time- Automatic payments should be your friend. Set up an account strictly for your bills and set up autopay.

2. Using the snowball effect is an effective way to pay off your credit card balances (instructions Included on how to do this)

3. Old accounts in good standing keep them open closed account with age and good history let them be do not have them removed unless it contains negative erroneous information.

4. Piggybacking is another strategy to build positive credit history if there is someone you trust that has a CC account with good history & on time payment with good Utilization Have them add you as an authorized used on their CC and you will adopt all of these positive history.

---

5. Starting a Self-lender credit builder account at www.selflender.com is a wonderful way to build and save at the same time. This option may also be available at your local back

6. Applying for a secured CC is another way to build a few recommended companies would be Discover, Capitol One, or Open Sky. This option may also be available through your local bank as well

> A. Choosing a card according to your score is important
> B. 550-Under secured cards with no credit check
> C. 550-580-Secured cards Capitol one, Discover, Credit One etc.…
> D. 580-680-Walmart, Capital One, Barclay Store Cards
> E. 680-750 Capital One, Barclay Store Cards, Discover, Amex, Chase
> F. 750-above without negative history you're fine for all

7. A strong credit report has a mix of types of credit, installment accounts, revolving accounts… etc. this makes up 10% of your score.

Note: Going forward monitor your reports regularly. Pay all accounts on time. Keep credit card utilization under 30%. Congratulations on your journey! making your goals a thing of the past.

Notes

Notes

Notes

____

____

____

____

____

____

____

____

____

____

____

Notes

Notes

Business Credit

Step 1: Obtain an EIN

An EIN is an Employer Identification Number and is issued by the IRS. There is no fee to apply for an EIN from the IRS. You want to research different business structures before applying.

Also, make sure the name you choose for your business is available in the state you are registering your business.

You will need an address for your business that is not a residential address, most creditors will deny you for having a residential address if you are a business. If you are truly working from home, I will suggest a virtual office. I will provide a list of suggestions in our resources page.

Step 2: Register your business with your state

Before you obtain your EIN, you will want to research the different business structures. There a 4 main business structures, Sole Proprietors, Partnership, Limited Liability Company, and Corporation. Most entrepreneurs choose a Sole Proprietors as their business structure, while that is perfectly legal and fine, it does not protect the business owner personal assets.

Step 3: Apply for your Duns & Bradstreet Number

This is key to establishing business credit, without your D&B number you cannot generate a business score for business credit.

Obtaining your D&B number is totally FREE, please do not pay to obtain this number, it takes about a month to get your number assigned to you. However, you can pay to expedite the process which is at your discretion.

Step 4: Online Presence

Next you will need to create a website and obtain a professional email address for your business. Most creditors will use this as a factor to determine your eligibility. You can purchase a domain and hosting company from GoDaddy, they also offer professional email accounts. There are other companies available, but I have found GoDaddy to be start-up friendly. They are always having a sale.

Step 5: Communication

Obtain a business phone number and fax number, it must be listed and not a cell phone. There are a few companies that provides telephone and fax numbers for monthly fees. Also please get your business listed in directories, it will validate your presence offline.

Step 6: Apply for credit/vendors

After all the above is completed, you are now ready to start applying for accounts to establish a Paydex score.

You should start with Net30 accounts, as it is easier to obtain credit from them. All you must do is place an order and select invoice me/bill me later. These accounts are tier 1 and if they report to the credit bureaus, you will establish a Paydex score. Please keep in mind that it is ideal to have 5 of these accounts, to establish a Paydex Score.

Once you have a Paydex score, you can move on to Tier 2 accounts. Please remember that you must use your purchasing power wisely, to make this beneficial for your business.

When ordering do not order in amounts you know you cannot repay within the payment terms. Your full balance will be due 30 days from your order date, but it will benefit you to pay between 5-10 days before your due date.

Resources

EIN: www.irs.gov/businesses/small-businesses-self-employed/apply-for-an-employer-identificationnumber-ein-online

EIN: www.foxbusiness.com/features/2013/01/31/five-reasons-why-small-business-shouldincorporate.html

Virtual Address:

www.anytimemailbox.com
www.regus.com
www.alliancevirtualoffices.com

Website:

www.godaddy.com
www.wix.com
www.weebly.com

Phone & Fax:

www.onesuite.com
www.grasshopper.com
www.ringcentral.com

Vendors

Tier I Vendors- Establish as many of these accounts as possible net 30 or revolving and make purchases with onetime payments to start building your credit file. Normally accomplished 0-6 months some accounts can be established by calling or online. Do not PG on any of these accounts use just your EIN/Duns number

1.   **Uline**

2.   **Quill**

3.   **Grainger**

4.   **Ben Meadows**

5.   **HD Supply**

6.   **Hardware Express**

7.   **Seton**

8.   **Advance Auto Parts**

9.   **Interstate Batteries**

10.   **O" Reilly**

11.   **Blue Ribbon Web Hosting**

12.   **Global Industrial**

13.   **Monopolize Your Marketplace**

14.   **Supply Works**

15.   **FedEx**

16.   **NTB Tire**

17.   **Amsterdam Printing**

18.   **Kinkos Commercial**

Tier II Vendors- Before applying to these accounts listed below you should have at least 5-10 accounts from the list above reporting on your D&B Credit File & Experian Credit file for a minimum of 6 months or more with a Paydex score of 80+ with good reporting credit history for best results do not PG for any accounts listed below you use your EIN/D&B number

1. **Lands' End**
2. **Office Depot Business**
3. **AW Direst**
4. **Valero**
5. **Citi Bank gas cards Commercial**
6. **Pilot Flying J**
7. **Fleet Cor Commercial**
8. **Wex, Loves Universal Card, WaWa Universal Card. Fleet Corp Commercial**
9. **Shell gas card, Chevron and Texaco, Citgo**
10. **Sprint, Verizon Any Cell service**
11. **J C Penny Commercial**
12. **Northern Tool**
13. **Newegg**
14. **Amazon Revolving or Net 55**
15. **U-Haul Commercial**
16. **Sears Commercial**
17. **Sam's Club Commercial**
18. **Lowes Commercial**
19. **Home Depot Commercial**
20. **Ryder**
21. **Enterprise**

Tier III-Vendors- Before applying for the accounts listed below the steps for tiers 1&2 should be completed with at least 10 or more accounts reporting in good standing with a Paydex score of 80+ or more and a personal Credit score of at least 680 or higher with at least 12 months of continuous on time payments and reporting for both your business and personal credit to achieve the best results. For some of these accounts listed you will have to be a Personal Guarantor (PG)

1. **Capitol One Corporate Card**

2. **Capitol one Spark**

3. **Home Depot new 30/ Revolving**

4. **Apple Lease**

5. **Dell**

6. **Key Bank**

7. **Wright Express**

8. **American Express**

9. **Ally**

10. **Ford Motor Credit**

11. **Nissan**

12. **Toyota**

13. **Auto flex Leasing**

14. **D&M Auto Leasing**

15. **Benz**

16. **Bank Business Loans**

17. **Funding Loans (Watch out for the legalized loan sharks giving you working capital and debiting your account daily or weekly)**

<u>Note</u>

<u>Notes</u>

<u>Notes</u>

Budgeting

Budgeting is an essential financial skill everyone needs to understand and implement in their lives in order to be successful. It addresses your financial situation and distinguish between your needs and wants.

What is a budget?

A budget is a financial plan that takes income and expenses into ac

count and provides a visual of your money and its potential.

How Do I Budget?

Follow these steps to create a basic budget for you

Step 1. Create a list of the money you receive monthly. This includes everything from employment to residual income

Step 2. Create a list of the money you spend monthly. This includes bills and luxuries.

Step 3 Subtract what you spend monthly from what you receive monthly. Do you have any money left over? If you do that is a good sign, if not then you really need to start budgeting.

Step 4. Prioritize your spending habits, eliminate any unnecessary bills you have allocated or things you spend your money on.

Step 5. Save money you have left over to start an emergency fund and for your future goals.

We have provided templates for you to utilize in assisting you with creating a budget.

Monthly Simple Budget Worksheet

		Actual Amount	Budget Amount	Difference	Notes
__________ Monthly Budget					
	Bills				
Income					
Income 1					
Income 2					
Income 3					
Income 4					
Income 5					
Income 6					
Income 7					
Total					
Expenses					
Fixed Expenses					
Variable Expenses					
Savings					
Personal Savings					
Emergency Fund					
Other					

Savings

Having a savings plan and account provides a sense of security. There is no way to predict the future and nothing is guaranteed, in order to protect ourselves and our families we must save. Saving is also good for accomplishing goals as well, when funding is needed.

What is savings?

Savings is the act of being financially responsible by putting money aside for the future.

How Do I Save?

Here are some tips for you to begin saving.

Tip 1. Budget your money weekly and eliminate unnecessary spending habits.

Tip 2. Every time you receive money put 10% of it to the side for your savings account.

Tip 3. Open an online savings account for you to deposit your savings. It will be hard to gain access to those funds

Tip 4. Deduct money from your payroll check automatically between 5%-15%

Tip 5. Have more than one source of income. Find a way to make additional money outside of your primary income source.

We have provided savings challenges for you to start you off on your savings journey.

30 Day Money Challenge
Save nearly $500 in 30 Days

Day	Deposit	Balance	Day	Deposit	Balance
1	$1	$1	16	$16	$136
2	$2	$3	17	$17	$153
3	$3	$6	18	$18	$171
4	$4	$10	19	$19	$190
5	$5	$15	20	$20	$210
6	$6	$21	21	$21	$231
7	$7	$28	22	$22	$253
8	$8	$36	23	$23	$276
9	$9	$45	24	$24	$300
10	$10	$55	25	$25	$325
11	$11	$66	26	$26	$351
12	$12	$78	27	$27	$378
13	$13	$91	28	$28	$406
14	$14	$105	29	$29	$435
15	$15	$120	30	$30	$465

$5 Savings Challenge

Start of by saving $5, then increase the amount you save by $5 each week for a year. **$6,890**

Week	Deposit	Balance	Actual Deposit	Actual Balance	Week	Deposit	Balance	Actual Deposit	Actual Balance
1	$5	$5			27	$135	$1,890		
2	$10	$15			28	$140	$2,030		
3	$15	$30			29	$145	$2,175		
4	$20	$50			30	$150	$2,325		
5	$25	$75			31	$155	$2,480		
6	$30	$105			32	$160	$2,640		
7	$35	$140			33	$165	$2,805		
8	$40	$180			34	$170	$2,975		
9	$45	$225			35	$175	$3,150		
10	$50	$275			36	$180	$3,330		
11	$55	$330			37	$185	$3,515		
12	$60	$390			38	$190	$3,705		
13	$65	$455			39	$195	$3,900		
14	$70	$525			40	$200	$4,100		
15	$75	$600			41	$205	$4,305		
16	$80	$680			42	$210	$4,515		
17	$85	$765			43	$215	$4,730		
18	$90	$855			44	$220	$4,950		
19	$95	$950			45	$225	$5,175		
20	$100	$1,050			46	$230	$5,405		
21	$105	$1,155			47	$235	$5,640		
22	$110	$1,265			48	$240	$5,880		
23	$115	$1,380			49	$245	$6,125		
24	$120	$1,500			50	$250	$6,375		
25	$125	$1,625			51	$255	$6,630		
26	$130	$1,755			52	$260	$6,890		

Savings Challenge

$30 Savings Challenge

$30/Week for 1 Year = $1,560

Date	Week	Deposit	Balance		Date	Week	Deposit	Balance
	1	$30	$30			27	$30	$810
	2	$30	$60			28	$30	$840
	3	$30	$90			29	$30	$870
	4	$30	$120			30	$30	$900
	5	$30	$150			31	$30	$930
	6	$30	$180			32	$30	$960
	7	$30	$210			33	$30	$990
	8	$30	$240			34	$30	$1,020
	9	$30	$270			35	$30	$1,050
	10	$30	$300			36	$30	$1,080
	11	$30	$330			37	$30	$1,110
	12	$30	$360			38	$30	$1,140
	13	$30	$390			39	$30	$1,170
	14	$30	$420			40	$30	$1,200
	15	$30	$450			41	$30	$1,230
	16	$30	$480			42	$30	$1,260
	17	$30	$510			43	$30	$1,290
	18	$30	$540			44	$30	$1,320
	19	$30	$570			45	$30	$1,350
	20	$30	$600			46	$30	$1,380
	21	$30	$630			47	$30	$1,410
	22	$30	$660			48	$30	$1,440
	23	$30	$690			49	$30	$1,470
	24	$30	$720			50	$30	$1,500
	25	$30	$750			51	$30	$1,530
	26	$30	$780			52	$30	$1,560

Snowball Effect

What is the snowball effect?

The snowball effect is a process to eliminate debt by aggressively paying off your debt one bill at a time. The thought is to choose the debt with the smallest balance and pay it off or pay as much as you can on it, while paying the minimum balance on your other bills.

For an example you have 3 bills, the balances and minimum payments for each bill is as follows:

Bill 1 $625 $15
Bill 2 $ 1000 $25
Bill 3 $800 $20

Since Bill 1 has the smallest balance, we will pay on this bill aggressively while only paying the minimum on the other bills. So, for this month we have an additional $275 to spare. We will pay the minimum payment for Bill 2 and Bill 3 and put the $275 on Bill 1 knocking the bill down from $625 to $350.

If we continue with this pattern, we will clear our debt faster than if we just paid the minimum balance on each bill. So, to make this successful, we will need to budget our money and cut back on our spending to produce the "extra funds" to put towards the bill we are working aggressively on to eliminate.

Do not stress yourself if you are only able to afford to make an additional payment of an extra $5 It is still progress!

Snowball Effect

Bills	Balance	Minimum Due	Amount Paid	New Balance

Snowball Effect

Bills	Balance	Minimum Due	Amount Paid	New Balance

Snowball Effect

Bills	Balance	Minimum Due	Amount Paid	New Balance

Snowball Effect

Bills	Balance	Minimum Due	Amount Paid	New Balance

Snowball Effect

Bills	Balance	Minimum Due	Amount Paid	New Balance

Snowball Effect

Bills	Balance	Minimum Due	Amount Paid	New Balance

Snowball Effect

Bills	Balance	Minimum Due	Amount Paid	New Balance

Snowball Effect

Bills	Balance	Minimum Due	Amount Paid	New Balance

Snowball Effect				
Bills	**Balance**	**Minimum Due**	**Amount Paid**	**New Balance**

Snowball Effect

Bills	Balance	Minimum Due	Amount Paid	New Balance

Snowball Effect

Bills	Balance	Minimum Due	Amount Paid	New Balance

Snowball Effect

Bills	Balance	Minimum Due	Amount Paid	New Balance

Social Media Marketing Strategy

____
Month

____
Topic of the month

Topic:

- o _______________________________
- o _______________________________
- o _______________________________
- o _______________________________

Freebie:

- o _______________________________
- o _______________________________
- o _______________________________

Basic Product/Service:

- o _______________________________
- o _______________________________
- o _______________________________

Premium Product/Service:

- o _______________________________
- o _______________________________
- o _______________________________

Ultimate Product/Service

- o _______________________________
- o _______________________________
- o _______________________________
- o _______________________________

Social Media Marketing Strategy

____
Month

____
Topic of the month

Topic:

- o ______________________________
- o ______________________________
- o ______________________________
- o ______________________________

Freebie:

- o ______________________________
- o ______________________________
- o ______________________________

Basic Product/Service:

- o ______________________________
- o ______________________________
- o ______________________________

Premium Product/Service:

- o ______________________________
- o ______________________________
- o ______________________________

Ultimate Product/Service

- o ______________________________
- o ______________________________
- o ______________________________
- o ______________________________

Social Media Marketing Strategy

____
Month

____
Topic of the month

Topic:

- O _______________________
- O _______________________
- O _______________________
- O _______________________

Freebie:

- O _______________________
- O _______________________
- O _______________________

Basic Product/Service:

- O _______________________
- O _______________________
- O _______________________

Premium Product/Service:

- O _______________________
- O _______________________
- O _______________________

Ultimate Product/Service

- O _______________________
- O _______________________
- O _______________________
- O _______________________

Social Media Marketing Strategy

____
Month

____
Topic of the month

Topic:

- O _______________________________
- O _______________________________
- O _______________________________
- O _______________________________

Freebie:

- O _______________________________
- O _______________________________
- O _______________________________

Basic Product/Service:

- O _______________________________
- O _______________________________
- O _______________________________

Premium Product/Service:

- O _______________________________
- O _______________________________
- O _______________________________

Ultimate Product/Service

- O _______________________________
- O _______________________________
- O _______________________________
- O _______________________________

Social Media Marketing Strategy

____
Month

____
Topic of the month

Topic:

- ___________________________________
- ___________________________________
- ___________________________________
- ___________________________________

Freebie:

- ___________________________________
- ___________________________________
- ___________________________________

Basic Product/Service:

- ___________________________________
- ___________________________________
- ___________________________________

Premium Product/Service:

- ___________________________________
- ___________________________________
- ___________________________________

Ultimate Product/Service

- ___________________________________
- ___________________________________
- ___________________________________
- ___________________________________

Social Media Marketing Strategy

Month

Topic of the month

Topic:

- o _______________________________
- o _______________________________
- o _______________________________
- o _______________________________

Freebie:

- o _______________________________
- o _______________________________
- o _______________________________

Basic Product/Service:

- o _______________________________
- o _______________________________
- o _______________________________

Premium Product/Service:

- o _______________________________
- o _______________________________
- o _______________________________

Ultimate Product/Service

- o _______________________________
- o _______________________________
- o _______________________________
- o _______________________________

Social Media Marketing Strategy

____

Month

____

Topic of the month

Topic:

- o _______________________________
- o _______________________________
- o _______________________________
- o _______________________________

Freebie:

- o _______________________________
- o _______________________________
- o _______________________________

Basic Product/Service:

- o _______________________________
- o _______________________________
- o _______________________________

Premium Product/Service:

- o _______________________________
- o _______________________________
- o _______________________________

Ultimate Product/Service

- o _______________________________
- o _______________________________
- o _______________________________
- o _______________________________

Social Media Marketing Strategy

____
Month

____
Topic of the month

Topic:

- O _______________________________
- O _______________________________
- O _______________________________
- O _______________________________

Freebie:

- O _______________________________
- O _______________________________
- O _______________________________

Basic Product/Service:

- O _______________________________
- O _______________________________
- O _______________________________

Premium Product/Service:

- O _______________________________
- O _______________________________
- O _______________________________

Ultimate Product/Service

- O _______________________________
- O _______________________________
- O _______________________________
- O _______________________________

Social Media Marketing Strategy

____
Month

____
Topic of the month

Topic:

- ○ ______________________________
- ○ ______________________________
- ○ ______________________________
- ○ ______________________________

Freebie:

- ○ ______________________________
- ○ ______________________________
- ○ ______________________________

Basic Product/Service:

- ○ ______________________________
- ○ ______________________________
- ○ ______________________________

Premium Product/Service:

- ○ ______________________________
- ○ ______________________________
- ○ ______________________________

Ultimate Product/Service

- ○ ______________________________
- ○ ______________________________
- ○ ______________________________
- ○ ______________________________

Social Media Marketing Strategy

____

Month

____

Topic of the month

Topic:

- ○ ______________________________
- ○ ______________________________
- ○ ______________________________
- ○ ______________________________

Freebie:

- ○ ______________________________
- ○ ______________________________
- ○ ______________________________

Basic Product/Service:

- ○ ______________________________
- ○ ______________________________
- ○ ______________________________

Premium Product/Service:

- ○ ______________________________
- ○ ______________________________
- ○ ______________________________

Ultimate Product/Service

- ○ ______________________________
- ○ ______________________________
- ○ ______________________________
- ○ ______________________________

Social Media Marketing Strategy

____
Month

____
Topic of the month

Topic:

- ○ _______________________________
- ○ _______________________________
- ○ _______________________________
- ○ _______________________________

Freebie:

- ○ _______________________________
- ○ _______________________________
- ○ _______________________________

Basic Product/Service:

- ○ _______________________________
- ○ _______________________________
- ○ _______________________________

Premium Product/Service:

- ○ _______________________________
- ○ _______________________________
- ○ _______________________________

Ultimate Product/Service

- ○ _______________________________
- ○ _______________________________
- ○ _______________________________
- ○ _______________________________

Social Media Marketing Strategy

____
Month

____
Topic of the month

Topic:

- ○ _______________________
- ○ _______________________
- ○ _______________________
- ○ _______________________

Freebie:

- ○ _______________________
- ○ _______________________
- ○ _______________________

Basic Product/Service:

- ○ _______________________
- ○ _______________________
- ○ _______________________

Premium Product/Service:

- ○ _______________________
- ○ _______________________
- ○ _______________________

Ultimate Product/Service

- ○ _______________________
- ○ _______________________
- ○ _______________________
- ○ _______________________

________ Monthly Budget	Bills	Actual Amount	Budget Amount	Difference	Notes
Income					
Income 1					
Income 2					
Income 3					
Income 4					
Income 5					
Income 6					
Income 7					
Total					
Expenses					
Fixed Expenses					
Variable Expenses					
Savings					
Personal Savings					
Emergency Fund					
Other					

Monthly Budget

	Bills	Actual Amount	Budget Amount	Difference	Notes
Income					
Income 1					
Income 2					
Income 3					
Income 4					
Income 5					
Income 6					
Income 7					
Total					
Expenses					
Fixed Expenses					
Variable Expenses					
Savings					
Personal Savings					
Emergency Fund					
Other					

| | | Actual | Budget | | |
	Bills	Amount	Amount	Difference	Notes
Income					
Income 1					
Income 2					
Income 3					
Income 4					
Income 5					
Income 6					
Income 7					
Total					
Expenses					
Fixed Expenses					
Variable Expenses					
Savings					
Personal Savings					
Emergency Fund					
Other					

The table is titled "__________ Monthly Budget" across the top.

_____________ Monthly Budget				
	Bills	Actual Amount	Budget Amount	Difference	Notes
Income				
Income 1				
Income 2				
Income 3				
Income 4				
Income 5				
Income 6				
Income 7				
Total				
Expenses				
Fixed Expenses				
Variable Expenses				
Savings				
Personal Savings				
Emergency Fund				
Other				

	Bills	Actual Amount	Budget Amount	Difference	Notes
Income					
Income 1					
Income 2					
Income 3					
Income 4					
Income 5					
Income 6					
Income 7					
Total					
Expenses					
Fixed Expenses					
Variable Expenses					
Savings					
Personal Savings					
Emergency Fund					
Other					

_____________ # Monthly Budget

__________ Monthly Budget				
	Bills	Actual Amount	Budget Amount	Difference	Notes
Income				
Income 1				
Income 2				
Income 3				
Income 4				
Income 5				
Income 6				
Income 7				
Total				
Expenses				
Fixed Expenses				
Variable Expenses				
Savings				
Personal Savings				
Emergency Fund				
Other				

_____________ Monthly Budget

	Bills	Actual Amount	Budget Amount	Difference	Notes
Income					
Income 1					
Income 2					
Income 3					
Income 4					
Income 5					
Income 6					
Income 7					
Total					
Expenses					
Fixed Expenses					
Variable Expenses					
Savings					
Personal Savings					
Emergency Fund					
Other					

___________ Monthly Budget

	Bills	Actual Amount	Budget Amount	Difference	Notes
Income					
Income 1					
Income 2					
Income 3					
Income 4					
Income 5					
Income 6					
Income 7					
Total					
Expenses					
Fixed Expenses					
Variable Expenses					
Savings					
Personal Savings					
Emergency Fund					
Other					

__________ Monthly Budget				
	Bills	Actual Amount	Budget Amount	Difference	Notes
Income				
Income 1				
Income 2				
Income 3				
Income 4				
Income 5				
Income 6				
Income 7				
Total				
Expenses				
Fixed Expenses				
Variable Expenses				
Savings				
Personal Savings				
Emergency Fund				
Other				

___________ Monthly Budget

	Bills	Actual Amount	Budget Amount	Difference	Notes
Income					
Income 1					
Income 2					
Income 3					
Income 4					
Income 5					
Income 6					
Income 7					
Total					
Expenses					
Fixed Expenses					
Variable Expenses					
Savings					
Personal Savings					
Emergency Fund					
Other					

	Bills	Actual Amount	Budget Amount	Difference	Notes
Monthly Budget					
Income					
Income 1					
Income 2					
Income 3					
Income 4					
Income 5					
Income 6					
Income 7					
Total					
Expenses					
Fixed Expenses					
Variable Expenses					
Savings					
Personal Savings					
Emergency Fund					
Other					

	Bills	Actual Amount	Budget Amount	Difference	Notes
____________ Monthly Budget					
Income					
Income 1					
Income 2					
Income 3					
Income 4					
Income 5					
Income 6					
Income 7					
Total					
Expenses					
Fixed Expenses					
Variable Expenses					
Savings					
Personal Savings					
Emergency Fund					
Other					

<u>Notes</u>

<u>Notes</u>

<u>Notes</u>

Notes

<u>Notes</u>

Disclaimer

No part of this workbook may be reproduced in any form or by any electronic or mechanical means, including information storage and retrieval systems, without permission in writing from the Authors. While every effort has been made to verify the information in this directory and ensure the validity and currency of the content, neither the authors nor their affiliates or partners assume any responsibility for errors, omissions or inaccuracies. All information contained herein has been verified as true and accurate at the time of publishing of this content. Congratulations and thank you for your wise decision to invest in your future as we stated before this book was made with you in mind. Keep pushing and your goal will become your accomplishments!

<u>Journal</u>

____

____

____

____

____

____

____

____

____

____

____

____

____

From Goals to Accomplishments!